A ROOKIE READER

STOP-GO, FAST-SLOW

By Valjean McLenighan

Illustrations by Margrit Fiddle

Prepared under the direction of Robert Hillerich, Ph.D.

CHILDRENS PRESS ®

CHICAGO

Library of Congress Cataloging in Publication Data

McLenighan, Valjean.
  Stop-go, fast-slow.

  (A Rookie reader)
  Summary: A short poem emphasizing the
concept of opposites. Includes word list.
    1. English language—Synonyms and antonyms—
Juvenile literature. [1. English language—
Synonyms and antonyms] I. Fiddle, Margrit,
ill. II. Title. III. Series
PE1591.M27   428.1   81-17080
ISBN 0-516-03617-3   AACR2

The opposite of go is stop.

The opposite of bottom, top.

The opposite of left is right.

When day is over, then comes night.

One plays seek, the other hides.

One says yes, the other no.

One likes summer, one loves snow.

If you go in, then he goes out.

If you say, "Smile!" why then he'll pout.

If you're a boy,

then she's a girl.

You have straight hair?

Hers must curl.

You behave. Your opposite

will make a scene or throw a fit.

Back and front, or back to back,
Here's an entertaining fact:

If I sit opposite to you,

then you are opposite me, too!

Some opposites are either-or,
Like true or false, and peace or war.

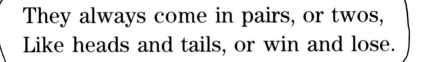

They always come in pairs, or twos,
Like heads and tails, or win and lose.

But still the earth keeps spinning.

WORD LIST

a	earth	here's
always	either	hers
an	end	hides
and	entertaining	I
anything	fact	if
are	false	in
back	fit	is
beginning	front	keeps
behave	full	left
bottom	girl	life
boy	go	like(s)
but	goes	lose
come(s)	hair	loves
curl	have	make
day	he	me
different	heads	must
do	he'll	night

no	scene	they
now	seek	throw
of	she's	to
one	sides	too
opposite(s)	sit	top
or	smile	true
other	snow	twos
out	spinning	war
over	some	way
pairs	still	when
peace	stop	why
plays	straight	will
pout	summer	win
reached	tails	yes
right	that	you
say	the	your
says	then	you're

About the Author

Valjean McLenighan, a graduate of Knox College in Galesburg, Illinois, became interested in writing children's books during her stint as an editor at a large midwestern publishing company. Since that time, many of her children's books have been published.

Though she nearly always has a book project in the works, Valjean finds time for a variety of other interests including the theater, children's television, the advertising business, and travel. She lives on the North Side of Chicago and enjoys spending time with her many friends in the Midwest and around the world.

About the Artist

A graduate of the Rhode Island School of Design, **Margrit Fiddle's** career has involved her in all aspects of the graphic arts. As creative director for a large midwestern publisher, she has supervised the design, layout, and printing of hundreds of children's books. She has designed catalogs, advertising, newsletters, and illustrated some children's books. "Grit" shares her newly purchased old house on the South Side of Chicago with three cats, which somehow just happen to appear here and there in *Stop-Go, Fast-Slow.*